WHO

THE HUMAN RELATIONS TRIAD

Exploring Identity, Empathy & Unity

D. W. YONCE

TRIAD LEADERSHIP PRESS

OCALA, FLORIDA

For permission requests, contact:

Triad Leadership Press
Ocala, Florida
www.TriadLeadershipPress.com
info@TriadLeadershipPress.com

ISBN (print): 979-8-9942311-0-4
ISBN (eBook): 979-8-9942311-1-1

Library of Congress Control Number: _____

Printed in the United States of America

First Edition
2025

Dedication

For those who serve, lead, and listen. For those who wear their uniform with dignity and respect. For those who question "who" with courage. And for every person working to turn division into connection.

Table of Contents

Front Matter

- A Note from the Author
- Epigraph
- Introduction
- Reflection

Part I - The Foundation of Human Understanding

Part II - The Practice of Human Connection

Closing

- Afterword: The Continuing Question
- Reflection
- Epilogue: Carrying the Question
- Acknowledgments
- About the Author
- Final Reflection

A Note from the Author

This book began as a question that followed me through every season of service: *Who?* Who am I in this moment? Who stands before me? And who are we together?

Over the years, that simple word guided negotiations, leadership decisions, and outreach conversations with people from every walk of life. The more I listened, the clearer it became that awareness, empathy, and unity are not abstract values; they are daily practices that define how we live and lead.

My hope is that these pages help you slow down long enough to see the people around you, and yourself with a little more understanding. That is where connection begins, and where every meaningful change starts.

Epigraph

"The beginning of wisdom is the definition of terms."
- Socrates

"Knowing yourself is the beginning of all wisdom."
- Aristotle

"Awareness builds empathy. Empathy builds unity. Unity builds strength."

Introduction

We spend our lives surrounded by people, yet many of us move through the world without ever truly understanding ourselves or one another. We respond to routines, expectations, pressures, and assumptions, often without pausing long enough to ask the question that quietly shapes every decision and every relationship: *Who?*

Who am I behind the roles I play, the history I carry, and the standards I try to uphold? Who are they beneath their fears, their differences, their strengths, and their stories?
And who are we when our lives intersect, when connection becomes more important than division or distance?

During my years of service, I stood beside people at both their strongest and most vulnerable moments. I witnessed how identity shifts under pressure, how empathy opens doors that judgment keeps closed, and how unity can emerge from even the most fragile circumstances. I also saw the weight people carry when they do not feel understood, valued, or seen.

This book exists because the question *"who"* is not simple.

> It is never finished.
> It evolves as we grow.
> It deepens as we listen.

It expands as we learn to see more of ourselves, and more of each other, with honesty and respect.

The Human Relations Triad was shaped not in theory, but in real encounters: in conversations on cold sidewalks, in homes filled with grief or hope, in teams learning to trust again, in communities seeking common ground, and in individuals whose pasts threatened to overshadow their futures.

From these experiences, I learned that three qualities matter deeply:

> **Honesty** - without it, identity becomes a performance.
> **Responsibility** - without it, growth never begins.
> **Respect** - without it, connection cannot hold.

Trust grows from these foundations, and unity emerges when we choose to practice them with intention.

This book invites you to examine *"who"* with patience, curiosity, and courage, not to judge, but to understand. Not to divide, but to connect. Not to reach perfection, but to deepen awareness: first of yourself, then of others, and finally of the space you share.

"Who" is the question beneath every conversation, every conflict, every misunderstanding, and every breakthrough? It is the question that brings clarity, the question that restores

connection, and the question that remains long after the answers change.

As you move through these pages, I hope you find not only insight, but encouragement to take the next step, to speak honestly, listen openly, act responsibly, and approach others with respect. Understanding *who we are* shapes *how we live,* and how we live shapes the world we create together.

The journey begins with a question, and that question is *"Who?"*

Reflection

Every meaningful journey begins with a moment of stillness, a pause long enough to notice who we are and who we are becoming.

Before you turn the page, take a moment to listen inward. Set aside the roles you carry, the expectations you manage, and the stories you have learned to tell.

Ask yourself, gently:
What part of me is ready to be understood?
What part of me is longing to be seen?
And what part of me is ready to grow into something more honest, responsible, and connected than before?

The Triad begins with awareness, is shaped by respect and honesty, and grows through every choice we make to understand ourselves and others more deeply.

This is your invitation not to rush ahead, but to begin with presence. Begin with curiosity.
Begin with *who*.

PART I

THE FOUNDATION OF HUMAN UNDERSTANDING

This section explores the origins of identity and relationship, the root of every connection.

Chapter 1

The Human Question

Theme: Every act of leadership, compassion, or conflict begins with one question: *Who are we in relation to one another?*
Purpose: To introduce identity as the foundation of all relationships.

Opening Context

Human connection begins not with strategy or skill but with self-recognition. Before trust is built or collaboration occurs, people silently assess identity: *Who am I? Who are they? Who are we together?* These three questions shape every conversation, decision, and relationship.

I learned that truth early in my law-enforcement career. One night, a routine call grew tense when two strangers, who did not know each other and barely knew me beyond the uniform, each decided who the others were before a single question was asked. In that moment, I realized that control and calm had less to do with commands and more to do with connection. When I slowed down and acknowledged who each of us was in that space, the conflict eased. That lesson stayed with me for the next forty-five years: until people feel seen, they rarely listen.

In a world marked by division, distraction, and digital distance, *who* often becomes blurred. Roles, labels, and titles substitute for authenticity. Yet the ability to lead, heal, or connect begins by returning to that original question.

This book is not a set of theories; it is an invitation to observe yourself and others more clearly. Through decades of leadership, conflict resolution, and community service, one truth has remained constant: misunderstanding *who*, lies at the core of every breakdown in trust and cooperation.

The Human Relations Triad restores that clarity. It begins with *I*, expands to *they*, and evolves into *we*.

Core Concept

Humans are relational beings. Every interaction, verbal or silent, carries identity at its core. When people say *I*, they reveal their sense of worth and belonging. When they say *they*, they define difference. When they say *we*, they reveal unity.

> If *I* is weak, insecurity distorts behavior.
> If *they* is misinterpreted, bias and assumption grow.
> If *we* is false, collaboration collapses under pressure.

The Triad offers a simple structure for understanding behavior: - identity → perception → relationship - Human connection is a progression, not an event.

Framework or Model

Who Am I - The Inner Foundation

Self-awareness, integrity, and purpose form identity. Without a stable "I," behavior drifts.

Who Are They - The External Perspective

Understanding others requires perception free of assumption. Empathy begins where bias ends.

Who Are We - The Relational Bridge

The space where cooperation, shared purpose, and partnership become possible.

These are not stages to complete but states to maintain.

> Awareness of *I* sustains authenticity.
> Awareness of *they* sustains respect.
> Awareness of *we* sustains unity.

When one weakens, the entire structure tilts.

Understanding Motive and Purpose

Every "who" carries a motive, the quiet force driving behavior, decisions, and reactions. Some motives grow from responsibility or hope; others arise from fear, insecurity, or a desire to protect what matters most. Motive is the engine behind movement, even when that movement appears small or uncertain.

Purpose gives motive direction. It reveals what a person is trying to achieve, preserve, repair, avoid, or become. When a motive aligns with a clear purpose, behavior becomes more consistent and relationships more predictable. When motive and purpose remain hidden or conflicted, misunderstandings multiply.

Taking the time to listen for someone's motive, and to see the purpose behind their actions or silence, allows us to understand them more fully. This awareness softens judgment, sharpens empathy, and strengthens connection, because behavior rarely makes sense until motive and purpose enter the picture.

Understanding "who" will always include understanding "why." Understanding "who" also means acknowledging that not every motive aligns with connection, and not every purpose is rooted in goodwill.

Application and Practice

Personal Reflection Exercise
Write three statements -"Who am I?", "Who are they?", "Who are we?"- and revisit them in personal, professional, and community settings. Notice alignment and disconnection.

Observation Practice

During interactions this week, notice which perspective you are operating from:

- *I* (self-protective or assertive?)

- *They* (observing or assuming?)

- *We* (collaborating or sharing responsibility?)

Dialogue Application

Reframe tension with *who* language. Instead of: "They don't understand the issue." Try: "Who are we in this conversation, and what are we trying to achieve?"

This simple shift moves attention from blame to belonging.

Leadership and Community Perspective

Leaders often ask, "What should I do?" when the real question is, "Who am I in this moment?" A grounded identity guides decisions under pressure. Unclear identity leads to reaction instead of response.

Communities face similar challenges. Divisions between agencies, generations, or social groups often arise from unclear identity and purpose. Restoring the *"who"* resets direction.

When volunteers, caregivers, or leaders view clients not as *they* but as *we*, trust expands and outcomes improve.

Summary and Anchor Thought

Understanding begins with a question, and *"who"* is the question beneath every choice, every relationship, and every moment of reflection. It invites us to look past habit and assumption and explore the deeper layers of identity, intention, and connection.

Identity is shaped, not fixed, but formed moment by moment and influenced by our past without being defined by it. When we approach others with respect and ourselves with responsibility, we create the conditions for trust, empathy, and unity to grow.

Every step of the Triad grows from this first inquiry. When we dare to ask *"who,"* we open the door to understanding. When we pause long enough to listen, we uncover truth. When we move with curiosity and intention, we become wiser, steadier, and more connected.

Anchor Thought:
"To understand the world, first understand yourself within it."

Reflection

Every question begins with a moment of courage, and the question "Who?" is no different.

Pause and consider the first time you wondered who you were beyond expectations, history, and the roles that shaped you for so long they began to feel like identity itself.

Ask yourself:
What part of me have I not explored?
What truths am I ready to face with greater honesty?
What possibilities might open if I approached myself with the same curiosity I extend to others?

The journey continues each time we look inward with openness, patience, and the willingness to understand.

Chapter 2

Who Am I: The Inner Foundation

Theme: Identity is the root of human behavior.
Purpose: To explore self-awareness as the cornerstone of authenticity and emotional intelligence.

Opening Context

Every human interaction begins with self-definition. The way we think, listen, and respond reflects the story we carry about who we are. When that story is unclear or unstable, confusion spreads outward to teams, families, and communities.

Identity forms early but evolves throughout life. It is shaped by upbringing, environment, and experience, yet refined by reflection and choice. Many people mistake their roles for their identity. Roles change. Identity must endure.

Knowing "Who am I?" is not about ego; it is about alignment. It is the discipline of being internally consistent so that words, actions, and values operate in harmony. A strong inner foundation produces steadiness even in uncertainty. Before we explore *they* or *we*, we must stand firmly in *I*.

Self-Awareness

Self-awareness is the starting point of authenticity. It means noticing not just what we do, but why we do it. It is the pause that creates perspective.

I learned this during moments when decisions had to be made in seconds. Early in my career, I believed leadership was about control. Later, I realized it was about clarity. When I stopped reacting to what happened around me and started observing what was happening within me, my decisions changed. Awareness didn't make those choices easier, but it made them truthful.

Responsibility: Owning Who We Are

Identity is not only discovered; it is shaped through responsibility. Responsibility is the quiet acknowledgment that our choices, behavior, and direction belong to us.

When we accept responsibility:

- we choose intention over reaction

- we stop drifting and begin deciding

- we honor our values and our limits

- we act with integrity even when unseen

- we grow through humility when mistakes arise

9

Without responsibility, identity becomes fragile, a patchwork of excuses rather than a foundation of truth.

Owning our part in both success and struggle clarifies who we are today and opens the path toward who we can become tomorrow.

Honesty: The Foundation Beneath Identity

Honesty shapes identity from within. It asks us to speak truth not only to others but to ourselves.

When we pretend, hide, or explain away our choices, we disconnect from our own sense of self. Dishonesty forces us to *maintain* our story instead of *live* it, and each distortion requires another.

Living truthfully is simpler, lighter, and more humane. It frees us to show up as the same person in every room, relationship, and season.

Honesty also strengthens connection. People trust what is genuine, clarity over confusion, transparency over performance, sincerity over fear.

Identity grows when honesty guides it. Without honesty, identity becomes guesswork. Without it, relationships cannot hold the weight of real connection.

Self-Concept, Self-Expression, Self-Respect, Self-Actualization

- **Self-Concept** aligns belief with truth rather than assumption.

- **Self-Expression** reveals identity through behavior; when we live our truth, communication gains credibility.

- **Self-Respect** reminds us we are responsible for the standards we uphold and the boundaries we maintain.

- **Self-Actualization** is not perfection but congruence, the ongoing alignment of values and action.

Motive and Purpose Within Identity

Identity becomes clearer when we recognize what motivates us and why. Motive is the internal force behind our choices, the desire to belong, to achieve, to protect, to feel secure, or simply to be seen. Purpose directs that motive. It answers the deeper question: *What is my movement for?*

When motive and purpose align with our values, identity strengthens. When they drift apart, identity becomes conflicted. A person may act from fear while hoping for acceptance, or speak with confidence while feeling unsteady inside. These internal contradictions are signals that identity needs attention.

Understanding what motivates us, and the purpose behind that motivation, helps us make choices with greater integrity. It clarifies why certain patterns repeat and why some decisions feel right while others feel misaligned. When we are honest about motive and intentional about purpose, we begin shaping a truer version of ourselves. Identity grows stronger when built on conscious motive and meaningful purpose.

Summary and Anchor Thought

Identity is not something we find, it is something we shape. It grows through the choices we make, the values we honor, and the honesty and responsibility we bring to our own lives.

Honesty deepens identity. Responsibility anchors it. Together, they create the foundation for who we are becoming.

Anchor Thought:
"Honesty is the courage to face who we truly are, and responsibility is the decision to participate in who we become."

Reflection

Honesty is the quiet conversation we hold with ourselves before we ever speak a word to the world.

Pause and consider where your truth lives: in your values, your choices, your fears, and the stories you tell yourself to feel safe.

Ask yourself:
Where am I aligned with who I truly am?
Where have I drifted because silence felt easier than truth?

Every act of honesty strengthens identity. Every step toward truth makes connection possible. Honesty begins within, and from there, everything grows.

Chapter 3

The Shaping of Identity

Theme: Identity is both discovered and constructed.
Purpose: To explain how external forces shape identity and how reflection reclaims authorship.

Opening Context

No one begins life with a blank page. From our earliest days, identity is shaped by the voices, expectations, and environments around us. Before we learn to define ourselves, others begin writing the first chapters of our story. Family values, cultural norms, early roles, and meaningful experiences shape the foundation of "who I am."

This shaping offers belonging and direction, but it can also create limitations. We internalize judgments, fears, and expectations that may no longer serve us. Many adults live within stories they did not write and have never questioned.

To understand identity is to reclaim authorship. Maturity requires distinguishing what was inherited from what was chosen. Growth requires recognizing influence without surrendering control.

Across forty-five years in uniform and public service, I witnessed how identity evolves. Early mentors shaped my discipline. Later colleagues shaped my patience. Experiences shaped my perspective. But none of these fully defined me. Real leadership began when I realized that I could choose which influences to carry forward and which ones to release. That was the moment my identity became my own.

This chapter explores how identity is formed, distorted, and ultimately rewritten through awareness and intention.

Core Concept

Human identity is dynamic, a living combination of inheritance, experience, and choice. We absorb culture and conditioning long before we recognize them. Later, reflection allows us to examine those inputs, refine them, and sometimes rewrite them. Identity develops through three interacting forces:

1. **Formation** - the early imprint of family, community, and culture.

2. **Reinforcement** - feedback loops that strengthen self-beliefs.

3. **Revision** - conscious editing and redefinition as awareness deepens.

Identity is the balance between belonging and autonomy.

The Five Shapers of Identity

1. **Family**

    Early messages, spoken and unspoken, shaped worth, belonging, and possibility. Childhood patterns echo into adulthood unless examined.

2. **Culture**

    Norms, values, and expectations influence what we believe is acceptable or admirable. Culture can expand or restrict identity.

3. **Experience**

    Success, failure, trauma, and growth leave emotional and cognitive imprints that affect future choices.

4. **Environment**

    Workplaces, communities, and relationships reinforce or challenge self-perception.

5. **Choice**

    The most powerful shaper of all. At any point in life, we can choose what beliefs to keep and what to release.

Application and Practice

Reflection Exercise - Inherited vs. Chosen
List five beliefs you hold about yourself. Mark each one as *Inherited* or *Chosen*. Notice which beliefs support your growth and which you may be ready to revise.

Awareness Exercise - Identity Triggers
When strong emotions arise, ask:
"Which part of my identity felt challenged?"
This builds emotional clarity.

Dialogue Exercise - Story Revision
Share one outdated belief about yourself with someone you trust. Naming the belief aloud begins the process of rewriting it.

Leadership and Community Perspective

In leadership, identity determines tone and credibility. Leaders who understand their own shaping, guide others without judgment. They recognize that behavior often grows from stories carried for decades, many of which can be rewritten.

Communities also carry inherited narratives. Some unify, others divide. Renewal begins when people examine which parts of their shared story still serve who they want to become.

Summary and Anchor Thought

Identity evolves through awareness and choice. When we understand what shaped us, we gain the freedom to shape ourselves.

Anchor Thought:

"What was learned can be relearned."

Reflection

Identity is shaped long before we recognize it, through moments we remember and moments we never realized were shaping us at all.

Pause and consider the pieces of your story: the people who influenced you, the challenges that strengthened you, the lessons you carried unknowingly, and the experiences that still echo today.

Ask yourself:
Which parts of my identity were chosen for me, and which have I chosen for myself?
What am I ready to keep, and what am I willing to grow beyond?

Each step toward understanding your story brings you closer to the person you are becoming.

Chapter 4

Who Are They: The External Perspective

Theme: Understanding others begins when perception gives way to curiosity.

Purpose: To explore perception, bias, empathy, and the humanization of "they."

Opening Context

Every human system, family, workplace, or community depends on how accurately people perceive one another. Most conflict arises not from malice but from misinterpretation. We see what our experience allows, then mistake that partial image for truth. "They" becomes shorthand for anyone outside our current circle.

But behind every "they" stands an individual as complex as "I." Human connection requires learning to replace assumption with observation.

In my work, I met people from every background imaginable, and one lesson remained constant: each person has a reason for the way they see the world. Early in my career, I sometimes judged behavior before understanding the story behind it. Over time, I learned to pause and ask, "What might they be carrying that I cannot see?" That single question changed everything. Seeing the person before the circumstance turned confrontation into conversation.

Working with the homeless deepened this understanding. No two people carried the same wound, the same hope, or the same story. Solutions could not be scripted. Real progress began only after we asked who they were and listened long enough for them to answer in their own way.

When perception is rigid, relationships harden. When curiosity re-enters, learning resumes.

Core Concept

Human perception is fast, automatic, and often inaccurate. The mind fills in gaps using three forces:

- **Perception** - filters shaped by emotion and experience

- **Projection** - attributing our fears or assumptions to others

- **Position** - the social or cultural distance shaping interpretation

Unchecked, these forces distort empathy and reinforce boundaries rather than truth.

Four Dimensions of "They"

1. **The Familiar vs. The Unknown**
   We trust what feels familiar. Yet every person we now trust was once a stranger.

2. **The Similar vs. The Different**
   Similarity feels safe; difference feels risky until understood. Curiosity bridges that risk.

3. **The Group vs. The Individual**
   We often see groups instead of people. Real connection always happens one person at a time.

4. **The Story We Tell vs. The Story They Live**
   We judge fragments. They live full stories. Understanding requires listening for context rather than assuming it.

Honoring the Differences That Shape "They"

Every person carries a different history, rhythm, and set of strengths and limitations. No one arrives from the same circumstances or the same starting line; yet every person deserves dignity, respect, and opportunity.

People learn at different speeds, in different ways, and through different experiences. Some have visible disabilities.

Others carry invisible ones. But disability never diminishes humanity, and difference never diminishes worth.

To understand "who they are," we must move beyond labels and expectations and meet people where they are, not where we assume they should be.

When we honor diverse paths, we see people not as problems to solve, but as individuals to understand. In that understanding, connection becomes possible.

Seeing the Motive Behind the Behavior

People rarely act without reason. Beneath every reaction is a motive, a fear being protected, a need being defended, a hope being pursued, or a wound being carried quietly. What we see on the surface is often only the expression of something deeper.

When we slow down long enough to look for motive, we shift from judgment to curiosity. And when we look for purpose, the direction someone is trying to move toward, we begin to understand the choices they make, Even when those choices appear confusing or contradictory.

Someone withdrawing may be trying to protect their dignity.

Someone growing quiet may be trying not to burden others.

Someone pushing back may be fighting for respect or

autonomy.

Someone hesitating may be navigating fear rather than defiance.

Understanding motive does not excuse harmful behavior, but it explains the human story behind it. Purpose reveals what a person is trying to regain, reclaim, or become.

When we take the time to see the motive and the purpose behind someone's actions or silence, empathy deepens and connection becomes possible. We begin to see not just what people do, but *why* they do it.

When Motive Turns Harmful

Not every motive is grounded in fear, protection, or hope. Some motives, as I witnessed throughout my law-enforcement career, are rooted in harm. People sometimes act with purposes that are:

- criminal

- unethical

- exploitative

- manipulative

- or intentionally destructive

These motives still have a story behind them, but the story does not excuse the behavior or reduce the need for accountability.

Understanding harmful motives is not about offering justification; it is about recognizing reality. Some individuals use their influence, knowledge, or position in ways that take advantage of others' vulnerability. Others act from greed, power, retaliation, or impulses shaped by long-standing patterns they never confronted.

Even in these situations, empathy does not eliminate responsibility. Instead, it allows us to see the full landscape, to understand risk, protect others, and respond with clarity rather than with ignorance.

Seeing the human behind the behavior does not mean ignoring the impact of the behavior. Discernment requires us to recognize when motive is harmful and to set boundaries that protect the dignity and safety of others.

Understanding "they" includes recognizing both their humanity and their accountability.

Respect: The Ground Where Understanding Begins

Respect recognizes inherent human worth, not earned by perfection, but grounded in presence, integrity, and humanity.

Respect:

- deepens empathy

- reduces assumption

- softens conflict

- builds trust

- and allows connection across differences

Respect must also flow inward.

Without self-respect, we lose our voice.

Without respect for others, we lose connection.

Without mutual respect, we lose unity.

When respect is present, the space between people becomes ground where understanding grows.

Application and Practice

Curiosity Pause

Before reacting, pause and ask:
"What might they be carrying that I cannot see?"

Three-Question Check

> What do I know?
> What am I assuming?
> What else could be true?

One-Person Principle

Engage one individual at a time, not a stereotype or group. This principle alone can repair years of misunderstanding.

Leadership and Community Perspective

> Leaders shape culture by how they treat "they."
> When leaders stereotype, teams divide.
> When leaders stay curious, teams adapt and grow.

Communities thrive when individuals learn each other's stories rather than judging from a distance. Policy may address groups, but compassion always begins person by person.

Understanding "they" begins with humility, the willingness to believe there is something you do not yet know.

Summary and Anchor Thought

Human connection strengthens when assumptions are replaced with curiosity. Seeing others clearly requires slowing down long enough to understand who they truly are.

Anchor Thought:
"Every person's path is different, but every person's worth is the same."

Reflection

Every person carries a story that no one else has lived.

Within those stories are challenges, strengths, hopes, and
quiet details shaping who they are today.

Pause and consider:
How often do we look past someone's differences
and forget that dignity is the one thing we all share?

Every path is unique.
Every pace is personal.
Every person holds value beyond measure.

When we honor the diverse paths people walk,
we create space for understanding, and the possibility of
deeper human connection.

Chapter 5
The Space Between Us

Theme: Conflict and misunderstanding live in the space between "I" and "they."

Purpose: To examine what happens when the link between self and others breaks, and how that space can be bridged.

Context

Between every two people lies a space, the invisible territory shaped not by distance, but by perception, emotion, and expectation. In that quiet space, trust is built or trust is broken. Connection narrows or widens. Understanding grows or collapses.

Most conflict does not arise from intention. It arises from how meaning travels through that space. A glance, a tone, an assumption, each can distort what the other person meant. Misunderstanding expands the distance before either person realizes it's happening.

Across my supervisory years, I watched this space expand and close thousands of times. Early on, I misread silence as defiance when it was actually hesitation. The moment I stopped assuming motive and started asking intent, communication changed. Once people recognized I was listening instead of judging, the distance shrank.

In families, workplaces, and communities, the space between people determines culture. When it narrows, cooperation flows. When it widens, silence and resentment take root.

This chapter explores what creates separation, what sustains it, and how to close the space without losing individuality.

Core Concept

The space between people is psychological, not physical. It is shaped by three elements:

1. Assumption

When information is missing, the mind invents a story. These stories often reflect fear, not truth.

2. Emotion

Emotion colors perception. Fear tightens the space. Pride hardens it. Insecurity distorts what we think we hear.

3. Communication

The only tool that can clear the space, yet often the first to fail.

When all three distort at once, relationships fracture. The goal is not to eliminate space, but to keep it open, breathable, and navigable.

Application and Practice

The Pause Before Reaction

Before responding, take one breath.
Ask: *"What story am I telling myself right now?"*

Clarifying Questions

Instead of assuming motive, ask:

- "Can you help me understand what you meant?"

- "Is that what you intended to say?"

- "How can we make sure we're aligned?"

Clarity prevents conflict.

Name the Space

When tension rises:
"I feel a gap here. Can we slow down a moment?"
This simple acknowledgment invites mutual reset.

Leadership and Community Perspective

Leaders who manage the space between themselves and others create cultures where people feel safe, respected, and understood. Leaders who ignore that space allow fear, gossip, and misinterpretation to fill it.

Communities behave the same way. When people assume the worst, distance grows. When they slow down, listen, and clarify, the space narrows and trust forms.

Managing the space between "I" and "they" is not a soft skill; it is a strategic discipline.

Summary and Anchor Thought

The space between us is always present but never fixed. It widens through assumption and fear; it narrows through clarity, empathy, and intention.

Anchor Thought:
"Bridges begin where walls end."

Reflection

Between every two people is a space shaped by stories, emotions, and unspoken meaning.

Pause and consider the spaces in your own life. The ones that feel tense, the ones that feel gentle, and the ones you wish were closer.

Ask yourself:
What assumptions might be living in that space?
What truth could reshape it?
And what small act of listening or patience might begin to bridge the distance between you and someone who matters?

Chapter 6

When Hope Breaks: Seeing the Person Behind the Pain

Theme: Hopelessness distorts identity and collapses connection.

Purpose: To understand how the Triad guides us when people lose their sense of self, their relationships, and their will to continue.

Opening Context

Hopelessness is one of the quietest yet most powerful forces in human life. It appears when a person no longer believes their presence matters, when the story they tell themselves becomes heavier than the situation they are living in.

Hopelessness collapses the *I*. It distorts *they*. And it makes *us* feel unreachable.

Many imagine hopelessness as loud or dramatic. More often, it is subtle: a withdrawn glance, a hesitant voice, a diminishing presence. When someone reaches this place, urgency is needed, but not the urgency of solutions. The urgency of awareness.

I have met people standing on the thin edge between holding on and giving up. Some were homeless neighbors who had lost the last thread of dignity they once carried. Others were officers, firefighters, veterans, caregivers, or parents hiding burdens behind their roles. In every instance, I learned that help begins long before intervention. It begins with presence, with slowing down long enough to see the person behind the pain.

Core Concept

Hopelessness occurs when all three parts of the Triad collapse:

Identity (Who Am I?) fails

Worth feels lost. Purpose disappears.
The person becomes a shadow of themselves.

Perception (Who Are They?) collapses.

Others feel unreachable, uninterested, or judged.

Connection (Who Are We?) dissolves.

Even surrounded by people, the person feels alone.

Hopelessness is not about circumstance alone. It is about identity, perception, and connection failing simultaneously.

Understanding *who* becomes the lifeline that reopens these doors.

Identity at the Edge

When hope fades, identity distorts:

> "I am a burden."
> "I am invisible."
> "I do not matter."
> "I am not who I used to be."

The person stops recognizing their own strength or potential. Small acts of connection can become more powerful than any major solution.

False Hope vs. Real Hope

False hope is quick reassurance that ignores reality:
> "You'll be fine."
> "Just stay positive."
> "It's not that bad."

Though well-intentioned, false hope deepens despair by invalidating truth.

Real hope is honest, grounded, and slow:
> "I'm here with you."
> "This is real, and you're not alone."
> "Let's take one step at a time."

Real hope honors identity.

The Stages of Complacency

Hopelessness almost never arrives suddenly, it erodes through:

1. Frustration - something painful happens.

2. Isolation - the person feels unseen or misunderstood.

3. Resignation - "Nothing will change."

4. Complacency - despair becomes familiar.

5. Withdrawal - the person detaches from others and from themselves.

Recognizing early signs creates opportunities for intervention.

Application and Practice

1. Slow Down Before Acting

Ask gentle, grounding questions:

>"What feels heavy right now?"

>"How long have you been carrying this?"

>"What would help you breathe easier in this moment?"

2. See the Person Behind the Pain

Identity often becomes the first casualty of despair. Remind them of who they are beyond what hurts.

3. Offer Realistic Support

Small, achievable steps rebuild confidence better than big promises.

4. Stay Present Without Pressure

Presence creates safety, while pressure creates distance.

Leadership and Community Perspective

Hopelessness appears everywhere: employees who have given up trying, seniors who feel forgotten, veterans living with invisible pain, teens overwhelmed by expectations.

Communities hold countless people quietly slipping from hope.

Leaders who are attentive to these early signals,
and who respond with humility rather than urgency,
help restore possibility long before crisis arrives.

Real leadership begins when someone slows down long enough to notice who is hurting.

Summary and Anchor Thought

Hope does not return through force or false reassurance.
It returns through presence, truth, patience, and identity.
Through someone willing to see the person behind the pain.

Anchor Thought:

"Hope begins where someone slows down long enough to see who you are."

Reflection

Hope rarely disappears in an instant; it fades quietly, often long before anyone notices.

Pause and reflect on moments when someone's pain was hidden behind silence, or when your own hope dimmed under the weight of uncertainty.

Consider what presence, patience, or understanding might have changed that moment.

And ask yourself:
Where can you be that steady presence now for yourself, or for someone whose hope is beginning to break?

Chapter 7

The Sixth Sense: What We Feel Before Words Begin

Theme: Human awareness extends beyond the five senses. The sixth sense helps us recognize emotional truth before it is spoken.

Purpose: To explore how instinct, presence, and intuitive perception help us understand people at their deepest levels.

Opening Context

Long before someone speaks, before they explain, defend, or describe, we often *feel* what is happening. This quiet internal awareness is one of the most powerful tools in human connection. It guides us when words fail, when pain is hidden, and when people are too overwhelmed or afraid to express themselves clearly.

The sixth sense is not mystical. It is profoundly human. It is experience sharpened over time, empathy attuned to subtle cues, and presence steady enough to notice the truth beneath behavior.

> We hear the hesitation behind an answer.
> We sense the heaviness in the room.
> We notice when a smile does not reach the eyes.
> We feel fear beneath a calm voice.

This awareness lives in the space between people.

I learned to trust this sixth sense long before I had a name for it. In uniform, it helped protect lives. Later, in outreach and crisis work, it helped reveal the person behind the pain. Some of the most important conversations of my life began with a simple inner whisper: *"Slow down. Something isn't right."* Those whispers were never loud, but they were always honest.

Core Concept

The sixth sense is emotional awareness that precedes understanding. It develops from three sources:

1. Experience

Patterns we have seen before become guidance for what we sense now.

2. Empathy

The ability to imagine someone's inner world, even when they cannot describe it.

3. Presence

The willingness to slow down, observe, and withhold judgment long enough to notice truth.

When the sixth sense is active, we notice:

- trembling hands

- quiet withdrawal

- practiced "I'm fine" responses

- abruptness that protects deeper fear

- silence that carries exhaustion or defeat

The sixth sense works only when paired with curiosity, humility, and compassion.

Interpreting What We Sense

The sixth sense is not about guessing, it is about noticing.

1. Emotional Tension

The body reveals stress long before words do: stiff shoulders, tight jaw, uneasy fidgeting.

2. Withdrawal

When someone is disappearing emotionally, they speak less, avoid eye contact, and minimize their needs.

3. Incongruence

Words say, "I'm okay," but everything else says otherwise. Tone, posture, and energy contradict the message being spoken.

The sixth sense often alerts us when someone's motives are not aligned with their words, even before we can explain why.

4. Abruptness

Quick responses or irritability often protect deeper pain.

5. Silence

Stillness is not always peace; sometimes it is exhaustion, fear, or defeat.

Recognizing these signals requires humility. We must approach people without assuming, diagnosing, or labeling. The sixth sense only works when paired with genuine curiosity.

Application and Practice

1. Slow the Moment

The sixth sense speaks only when we are quiet enough to hear it.

2. Ask Gentle Questions

- "You don't seem yourself today. What's weighing on you?"

- "I'm here. What do you need right now?"

- "Help me understand how you're feeling."

Questions open identity safely.

3. Match Their Pace

If they are fragile, be gentle.
If overwhelmed, be steady.

Presence communicates safety.

4. Listen With Your Whole Self

Listen to tone, pauses, contradictions, energy, silence.

5. Validate Their Reality

Validation rebuilds safety:
"I can see this is heavy."
"I hear you."
"Your feelings matter."

Leadership and Community Perspective

Leaders who rely on data alone often miss the most important information in the room: how people are *actually* doing.

The sixth sense helps leaders see:

- burnout before it erupts,

- fear before it shuts people down,

- isolation before someone disappears,

- conflict before it surfaces,

- despair before it becomes dangerous.

Strong communities depend on people who sense distress early and respond with humility rather than urgency. Parents, mentors, first responders, outreach workers, caregivers, supervisors, all carry the responsibility of awareness. The sixth sense is not optional. It is essential. When we learn to trust it, we learn to protect one another long before crisis arrives.

Summary and Anchor Thought

The sixth sense reveals who someone is beneath their words. It helps us detect pain, fear, or overwhelm before the person can voice it. When we honor this awareness, we create the space where connection and healing can begin.

Anchor Thought:
"What we feel before words begin, often tells us the truth we most need to hear."

Reflection

Some truths are not spoken, they are felt.

Pause and reflect on moments when you sensed more than someone said:

a hesitation…
a quiet shift in tone…
a look that lingered a bit too long…
a silence carrying its own message…

These subtle signals invite compassion.

Ask yourself:
Where might someone in your life be hoping you'll feel, what they cannot yet say? And how can you show up with the awareness that brings unspoken truth into the light?

Chapter 8

The Trust Bridge: The Currency of Human Connection

Theme: Trust is the invisible currency that determines the depth and durability of every relationship.

Purpose: To show how trust is built, broken, misused, restored, and essential to the Triad.

Opening Context

Trust is the foundation of all meaningful connection. It is the belief that another person's intentions and actions can be relied upon. It is the quiet sense of safety we feel when someone's presence steadies us. It is the comfort of consistency.

- But trust does not grow evenly.
- Some trust quickly.
- Some trust slowly.
- Some trust only after many tests.
- And some have learned through pain to guard themselves.

Throughout my years serving people in crisis, in uniform, in outreach, and in community support, I saw how trust behaves. Some individuals trusted within minutes; others needed ten encounters before believing help was real. But the lesson remained the same: **trust is not about speed, it is about consistency.**

One careless moment can undo months of connection. And once broken, trust is incredibly difficult to rebuild. Trust is not a feeling. It is a process, and understanding that process allows us to strengthen the bonds we depend on.

Core Concept

Trust is built through four essential elements:

1. Consistency

Steady, reliable behavior over time.

2. Honesty

Truth delivered with clarity and respect.

3. Competence

Follow-through. Ability. Dependability in action.

4. Care

The human warmth that makes trust feel safe.

When one element weakens, trust becomes unstable. When all four align, trust becomes a bridge strong enough to hold weight.

False Trust

False trust is trust built on:

- manipulation

- selective kindness

- charm without integrity

- dependency disguised as connection

- inconsistency masked as care

- emotional vulnerability exploited

- promises without follow-through

False trust feels like safety at first, but functions like a trap. It creates confusion, self-blame, and long-term harm.

False trust is more damaging than no trust at all because it teaches people to doubt their own instincts.

Rebuilding trust after false trust requires:

- patience

- presence

- honesty

- clarity

- consistent behavior over time

There are no shortcuts. Trust requires discernment, because not every motive deserves the same level of access to our confidence or vulnerability.

Trust Breaks

Trust breaks in two ways:

1. A Single Event

A betrayal, lie, or violation of safety.

2. Gradual Erosion

Small, repeated inconsistencies:

- broken commitments

- half-truths

- emotional withdrawal

- disregard

- unmet needs

- dismissive tone

Either way, the break is often sudden for the person who feels it.

How Trust Is Built

Trust grows through three practices:

1. Presence

Showing up, consistently.

2. Transparency

Clarity without cruelty.

3. Reliability

Doing what you say, especially in small things. Trust is built in ordinary moments long before crisis demands it.

Application and Practice

The Patience Principle. Some people need multiple encounters to trust. Consistency is the invitation; patience is the doorway.

The Clarifying Question
"Is there anything I've said or done that made you unsure of me?" Courageous - but transformative.

The Reliability Check
Say less.
Do more.
Let actions stabilize the connection.

The Boundary of Trust

Trust is earned, protected, and sometimes withdrawn for safety.

The Repair Step

Name the harm.

Take responsibility.

Show the change repeatedly.

Leadership and Community Perspective

Trust is what makes leadership legitimate.

> Not position.
> Not authority.
> Not title.

Trust shapes:

- teamwork

- family dynamics

- community cooperation

- conflict resolution

- crisis response

- organizational culture

Communities move toward unity when trust grows
and toward division when trust erodes.

Summary and Anchor Thought

Trust is the bridge that makes understanding possible.
It grows through consistency, honesty, competence, and care.
False trust harms; real trust heals. Trust is fragile, powerful,
and essential to "we."

Anchor Thought:
"Trust is the bridge we build slowly, and the one we must protect daily."

Reflection

Trust grows quietly, through small and steady moments.

Pause and consider:
Where has trust shaped your life?
Where might trust need to be rebuilt, within yourself,
with others, or between people who have drifted apart?

Trust begins with presence and is sustained through truth.

PART I

Closing Reflection

Every journey of understanding circles back to reflection.

Awareness leads us inward.
Empathy draws us outward.
Unity invites us to return with what we've learned.

The cycle never ends; it simply invites us to begin again
with greater patience, deeper vision, and renewed intention.

PART II

THE PRACTICE OF HUMAN CONNECTION

This section turns awareness into applied behavior, how to live, lead, and serve through the principles of the Triad.

Chapter 9

The Noise: Protecting Who We Are from What Surrounds Us

Theme: Noise - opinions, pressure, distraction, and false influence distort identity, perception, and unity.
Purpose: To help readers recognize external forces that interfere with clarity and connection.

Opening Context

Every day we live with noise, sometimes loud, sometimes quiet, always present. Noise is not merely sound. It is pressure, judgment, misinformation, emotional residue, comparison, and the constant stream of opinions that compete with our own inner truth.

Noise surrounds us in screens, headlines, comment sections, and conversations shaped more by reaction than reflection. It often influences decisions more deeply than actual circumstances. It distorts how we see ourselves, how we interpret others, and how we define "we."

Noise is dangerous because it impersonates truth. It blurs identity, amplifies insecurity, and divides communities before people ever meet.

Throughout my years of service, I watched individuals lose themselves in the weight of external voices, shaped not by fact, but by fear or influence. Families fractured by rumors. Communities misled by division. Vulnerable people pulled off course by those who never earned credibility.

Noise convinces us to stop listening to ourselves.

Understanding noise is essential to protecting identity and navigating relationships with clarity.

Core Concept

Noise interferes with all three parts of the Triad:

1. Noise distorts "Who Am I?"

It creates insecurity, comparison, confusion, and doubt. People lose confidence not because they changed, but because noise changed how they *saw* themselves.

2. Noise distorts "Who Are They?"

People interpret others through rumor, fear, and social pressure rather than truth.

3. Noise destroys "Who Are We?"

It divides groups, families, teams, communities, replacing curiosity with assumption and unity with conflict.

When noise grows louder than inner truth, identity weakens.

The Loudest Forms of Noise

1. Social Media Emotion
Platforms amplify outrage, comparison, and reactive thinking.

2. "They Say..." Culture
Anonymous influence carries no accountability, yet shapes real behavior.

3. Rumor & Misinformation
False stories travel faster and hit harder than truth.

4. Emotional Environments
Stress, conflict, and tension can shape us even when not directed at us.

5. Influence Without Credibility
Strangers online often influence more than trusted mentors.

Noise does not need evidence, only volume.

Noise and Personal Identity

Noise leads to:

- self-doubt

- hesitation

- identity confusion

- emotional instability

- abandoning personal values

When people lack clarity, noise chooses for them.

Noise nudges behavior slowly, shaping decisions over time until a person no longer recognizes the origin of their choices.

Noise and Vulnerability

People who are overwhelmed, discouraged, lonely, or searching for belonging are most vulnerable to noise. Noise promises quick answers and emotional certainty, but it replaces identity with influence.

Noise is easier to follow than your own truth is to protect.

Filtering the Noise

1. Ask: "Is this credible?"

> Not "Is it popular?"
> Not "Is it loud?"
> But "Is it *true*?"

2. Ask: "Does this align with who I am?"

Noise demands reaction.
Identity chooses response.

3. Ask: "Does this strengthen or weaken connection?"

If it divides without understanding, it is noise.

4. Ask: "Would I believe this if I were quiet?"

Silence reveals truth.
Noise hides it.

5. Limit exposure to unnecessary noise.

Your peace is not a public space.

Leadership and Community Perspective

Noise erodes:

- clarity

- unity

- empathy

- trust

- decision-making

- leadership presence

Leaders must model quiet confidence, filtering noise, grounding identity, speaking truth, and encouraging reflection.

Communities grow stronger when identity guides decisions instead of noise.

Noise divides, while clarity unites.

Application and Practice

1. Daily Quiet Check
Identify the voices you heard today.
Distinguish *your* voice from others.

2. Digital Boundaries
Protect emotional and mental clarity.

3. Re-center on "Who Am I?"
Return to values, purpose, and grounded relationships.

4. Reconfirm Sources
Influence should match credibility, not volume.

5. Practice Response, Not Reaction
Reaction fuels noise., while response builds meaning.

Summary and Anchor Thought

Noise is the external interference that competes with identity and connection. It distorts truth, weakens stability, and divides people before they ever meet. Filtering noise protects who we are.

Anchor Thought:
"Noise moves fast; truth waits for the quiet."

Reflection

Noise pulls us away from who we are.

Pause and listen inward:
What voices bring truth, and which bring confusion?
What influence needs to be released so your own identity
and purpose can be heard again?

Chapter 10

Communication: The Courage to Be Heard

Theme: Communication is the lifeline of human connection.
Purpose: To explore why communication matters, and why silence often harms more than conflict.

Opening Context

Communication is the heartbeat of every relationship. It is how identity becomes visible, how empathy becomes possible, and how unity becomes real. Without communication, people drift apart, not because they stop caring, but because they stop connecting.

> Communication is not noise.
> Noise confuses.
> Communication clarifies.
> Noise pressures.
> Communication creates safety.

Yet many of us struggle to speak.

> We stay quiet when words are needed.
> We avoid conversations that matter.
> We fear being misunderstood, rejected, or dismissed.
> We let silence build walls we never intended to build.

Across years of working with families, seniors, the homeless, and people in crisis, I saw the same pattern: most people were not struggling because they didn't care; they were struggling because they didn't communicate. Silence did the damage.

Honest communication is not about volume. It is about presence, clarity, and respect.

Core Concept

Communication strengthens all three parts of the Triad:

1. Communication strengthens "Who Am I?"

Speaking truthfully:

- validates identity

- clarifies values

- prevents resentment

2. Communication clarifies "Who Are They?"

Listening intentionally:

- prevents assumptions

- creates empathy

- reveals deeper motivations

3. Communication builds "Who Are We?"

Dialogue is the bridge between individuals.
Without it, connection collapses.

Why We Stay Silent

People stay quiet because they fear:

- judgment

- conflict

- hurting someone they care about

- revealing vulnerability

- appearing weak

- being ignored

- being misunderstood

Silence protects distance, not connection.

The Cost of Not Communicating

When communication stops:

- relationships weaken

- marriages drift

- teams misalign

- children feel unseen

- conflicts intensify

- loneliness grows

- unity dissolves

Silence is not peace. It is an unresolved question waiting in the space between people. Healthy communication depends not only on honesty, but on recognizing when another person's motive may not support open or safe dialogue.

Courage to Speak

Communication requires vulnerability.
It means saying:
> "This is how I feel."
> "This is what I need."
> "This is what hurt."
> "This is who I am."

Courage is not loudness; it is honesty.

Communication restores identity, invites understanding, and builds "we."

Listening: The Other Half of Communication

Most communication fails not because people won't speak, but because they won't listen.

Listening requires:

- attention

- humility

- presence

- openness

- empathy

Listening says:
"You matter."
"I see you."
"Your voice deserves space."

Listening is receiving another person's truth.

Practices That Strengthen Communication

Speak early and calmly.

Use clear "I" statements.

Practice gentle honesty.

Ask open-ended questions.

Create communication rituals.

Remove distractions.

Clarify before assuming.

Communication in Families

Families thrive on consistent communication. Children need it for confidence and emotional safety. Partners need it for understanding and shared direction. Silence fractures relationships long before conflict does. Communication keeps a family's heartbeat steady.

Communication in Leadership and Community

Leaders who communicate with clarity and empathy create stability. Teams respond to transparency. Communities heal when communication replaces assumption. Communication is the practice that turns awareness into unity.

Communication opens the door to connection, but connection grows only when we step forward with responsibility, courage, and intention. Many hesitate not because they lack desire, but because their past whispers louder than their future. Growth begins when we choose to participate in our lives again, to speak honestly, listen openly, and move toward the relationships and communities we hope to build. The next step in the Triad is not just understanding; it is applying that understanding with purpose.

Summary and Anchor Thought

Communication is the courage to be heard and the willingness to listen. It shapes identity, clarifies perception, and builds unity.

Anchor Thought:
"Silence protects distance; communication protects connection."

Reflection

Communication is the moment we choose connection over silence.

It invites us to listen with patience, speak with honesty, and trust that our presence matters.

Pause and consider what your communication reveals about who you are, who you care for, and who you are becoming.

Chapter 11
Practical Applications

Theme: Principles gain meaning only when practiced.
Purpose: To turn the Triad into daily behavior.

Opening Context

Understanding the Triad is only the beginning. Awareness, empathy, communication, and trust help us see ourselves and others clearly, but clarity alone does not create change. At some point, we must choose to step forward with responsibility, commitment, and drive.

This chapter explores how to turn insight into action: how to live the Triad in daily moments, how to apply it in relationships and leadership, and how to move beyond hesitation into purpose. Growth begins when understanding becomes practice. Knowledge without action fades.

Courage to Step Forward

Many people hesitate to take their next step. Some fear their past will interfere with their future; a mistake, a failure, a broken relationship, a painful chapter they can't forget.

Others worry that their choices have already defined them. They remain still, not for lack of ability, but because their past speaks louder than their possibility.

But the truth is simple:

We cannot control our past, but we own the responsibility for our future.

Growth begins the moment we stop standing on the sidelines of our own lives. Learning, curiosity, and willingness matter more than perfection. Confidence grows through experience. Wisdom grows through trying, failing, adjusting, and trying again. Courage is not the absence of fear, it is the decision to move forward despite it.

Responsibility, Commitment, and Drive: The Engine of Connection

Responsibility

Owning our choices, behavior, and influence. Responsibility strengthens identity and prevents blame from replacing growth.

Commitment

The discipline of showing up, following through, and staying present. Without commitment, trust collapses.

Drive

The internal motivation that turns awareness into action. Drive moves intention into motion and motion into transformation.

Together, these qualities make the Triad a *living* practice, not just a concept.

Balancing Empathy with Discernment

As we apply the Triad in daily life, it is important to remember that not every motive is healthy or constructive. While many people act from fear, uncertainty, or a desire to be understood, others may act from motives that are harmful, unethical, or intentionally deceptive. My years in law enforcement taught me that some motives aim to manipulate, exploit, or take advantage of another's trust. Empathy does not remove accountability, and understanding does not require us to ignore risk. Practical application of the Triad includes discernment, the ability to recognize when empathy must be paired with boundaries to protect ourselves and others from harmful intent.

Core Concept

Practical application follows three steps:

Awareness → Intention
Notice identity, emotion, purpose.

Intention → Behavior
Choose aligned action.

Behavior → Culture
Repeated actions shape relationships and environments.

Consistency matters more than complexity.

Three Practical Pathways

1. Personal Practice

Morning check-in: "Who am I today?"
Midday reflection: "Am I reacting or responding?"
Evening review: "Where did I align?"

2. Relational Practice

Ask open questions.
Listen more than you speak.
Affirm what matters to the other person.

3. Community & Team Practice

Begin with shared purpose:
"What are we here to accomplish?"
Distribute responsibility and celebrate collective wins.

Leadership and Community Perspective

The strongest teams are not those with the most talent, but those with the most trust. Communities thrive when everyday actions reflect awareness and empathy, not just policies. The Triad becomes powerful when practiced consistently by many people in quiet, intentional ways.

Summary and Anchor Thought

The Triad becomes real through daily behavior.
Awareness leads to empathy. Empathy leads to unity.
Unity creates strength.

Anchor Thought:
"Your past cannot direct your future unless you hand it the map."

Reflection

Fear often keeps us still, not because we lack ability, but because we doubt our right to move forward.

Pause and reflect:
What part of your past no longer needs to guide your future?
What step have you been avoiding?
What belief must shift so you can step into the life you are building?

Growth begins when you move toward possibility.

Chapter 12

The Evolving Self and Society

Theme: Personal growth and social progress follow the same path, awareness followed by responsibility.

Purpose: To show how the Triad scales from individuals to communities.

Opening Context

Every culture mirrors the consciousness of its people. The fears and beliefs that shape personal identity also shape institutions. When individuals stop asking *who*, societies drift toward division. When they start asking again, renewal begins.

History makes this clear: Growth follows reflection. Progress begins when a society looks inward honestly and chooses to evolve.

Through years in public service, I watched cities and organizations behave like individuals: pride before listening, division before empathy, healing after understanding. The Human Relations Triad offers a structure for this collective evolution.

Core Concept

Societies evolve through the same cycle as individuals:

1. Self-Reflection - Who Are We?

Communities examine identity, values, and history.

2. Understanding Others - Who Are They Among Us?

Differences become sources of learning.

3. Collective Unity - Who Are We Together?

Shared purpose shapes culture and progress.

When any part is ignored, fragmentation grows.

Three Layers of Collective Evolution

1. Personal Layer

Individuals anchor the entire process.

2. Relational Layer

Bridges form between groups when people listen to one another's stories.

3. Structural Layer

Institutions change when values and relationships change first. Communities mature when they recognize both the purposes that unite and the motives that undermine trust.

Community Reflection

Pick one issue facing your community. Ask:

> "Who are we in relation to this?"
> "Who is most affected?"
> "Who do we want to become?"

Dialogue Framework

Encourage people to share:

- a personal story

- a perception they held

- a realization they gained

Stories dissolve division.

Collective Purpose Alignment:

Unity begins in small circles.

Leadership and Community Perspective

Leaders guide the moral direction of communities.
When leaders model reflection and humility, communities follow. When leaders model division, communities fracture.

The Triad reminds us: Societal health is not measured by agreement, but by the ability to stay connected while navigating differences.

Summary and Anchor Thought

Societies evolve as individuals evolve. Awareness reveals truth. Empathy restores connection. Shared purpose creates unity.

Anchor Thought:
"A society matures when its 'we' becomes inclusive."

Reflection

As we grow, the world around us grows with us.

Pause and consider:
How has your view of yourself changed as you've learned to
see others more clearly?
What part of your community reflects your growth?
What part invites your continued presence and compassion?

Every small act of awareness shapes the larger story.

Chapter 13

What We Carry Forward

Theme: Human connection is both the foundation and fulfillment of life.
Purpose: To unite the three questions of the Triad into one lifelong practice.

Opening Context

The study of human relations returns to one enduring truth: we are never finished learning how to be human.

Each day presents a new mirror, a new "they," and a new chance to strengthen "we." Writing this book reminded me of how much the Triad shaped my life, long before I ever placed it into words. Each chapter brought forward people and moments that taught me the cost of awareness and the gifts of empathy. The process was humbling. It showed me how learning becomes a lifelong habit and how leadership, at its best, is simply service expressed through listening.

If these pages help others pause long enough to ask *who*, then every lesson from my years in service has found its purpose.

The Triad is not a checklist to complete; it is a compass that guides. It's three questions - *Who am I? Who are they? Who are we?*- keeps awareness active and connection honest.

Every return to these questions refines our understanding of self, others, and the purpose we share.

Core Concept

The Human Relations Triad is more than a framework, it is a way of living. Three lifelong practices sustain it:

Self-awareness (Who Am I?)

Pause, reflect, and choose integrity over reaction.

Empathy (Who Are They?)

Listen for the story before reacting to the behavior.

Unity (Who Are We?)

Repair distance, strengthen bonds, and act with collective responsibility. When practiced together, these habits reduce conflict, deepen relationships, and build resilient communities.

Putting the Triad Into Daily Life

At Home

> Awareness prevents reaction.
> Empathy softens tension.
> Unity strengthens bonds.

At Work

> Start meetings with "we" language.
> Encourage honest dialogue.
> Recognize contributions openly.
> Create a culture of shared purpose.

In Community

> **Bridge differences.**
> **Listen to unfamiliar stories.**
> **Help others find their missing "puzzle pieces," just as others once helped you find yours.**

Small, consistent actions shape long-term culture.

Leadership and Community Perspective

Leadership is strongest when it stays connected to humanity. Awareness without empathy becomes isolation. Empathy without unity becomes sentiment without progress. Unity without awareness becomes blind agreement.

True leadership balances all three. Communities thrive when people take responsibility for connection, choose cooperation over division, and remain committed to understanding. Community renewal begins with a shared question: *Who are we when we come together?*

Summary and Anchor Thought

Human maturity is not measured by how much we know, but by how deeply we understand ourselves, others, and our shared purpose.

Anchor Thought:
"Who we are becomes clear in how we treat others."

Reflection

Connection is both a practice and a promise.
When we listen before we speak and seek purpose beyond
ourselves, we keep the Triad alive in the ordinary work of
living.

In those small, daily motions, humanity finds its strength.

Chapter 14

Leadership in Motion

Theme: Leadership is not a position but a practice.
Purpose: To show how leadership emerges from the Triad in real time.

Opening Context

Leadership reveals itself not in title or authority, but in motion, in what leaders do, how they do it, and who they become in the process. Every leadership moment begins with the Triad:

> Who am I as I guide?
> Who are they as they follow, struggle, or grow?
> Who are we becoming through this interaction?

When leaders forget *who*, decisions become mechanical and relationships shallow. When they return to *who*, clarity and connection re-emerge.

Core Concept

Leadership shaped by the Triad follows three disciplines:

1. Identity Integrity (Who Am I?)

Understanding motives, values, and fears. Honest decisions inspire trust. Leadership requires the maturity to discern when someone's motive conflicts with the values or safety of the group.

2. Relational Understanding (Who Are They?)

Seeing each person's strengths, pressures, and potential. Empathy sharpens clarity and direction.

3. Shared Purpose (Who Are We?)

Creating a meaningful "we" increases engagement and strengthens culture. Shared responsibility drives performance.

Leadership thrives when these three disciplines remain balanced.

Leadership in Real Time

Leadership happens moment by moment:

Before the decision
"Who am I here? What guides my intent?"

During the interaction
"Who are they in this moment? What shapes their response?"

After the outcome

"Who are we now? What have we learned? How do we move forward together?"

This rhythm produces leaders who are grounded, responsive, and humane.

Application and Practice

Identity Calibration
Weekly reflection:

"What did I learn about myself this week?"
"Did my actions match my values?"
"Where did I react instead of respond?"

Empathy Work
Practice one "empathy pause" per day:

Listen to understand, not to direct.

Unity Actions
Begin conversations or meetings with shared-purpose language:

"Here's what we are working toward..."
"What do we need from one another?"
"How do we move forward together?"

Small language shifts create large cultural changes.

Leadership and Community Perspective

Leadership shapes the identity of groups, teams, and communities. The tone of a leader becomes the tone of the people.

When leaders practice the Triad:

- people feel safer

- communication opens

- trust deepens

- responsibility grows

- innovation increases

Communities fracture when leaders model division, and strengthen when leaders model connection.

Summary and Anchor Thought

Leadership begins with identity, grows through empathy, and is fulfilled in unity.

Anchor Thought:
"Leadership becomes strength when awareness builds connection."

Reflection

Leadership is not measured by authority. It is revealed in the moments when presence shapes a path forward.

Pause and reflect:
Where has your presence brought clarity or steadiness?
Which qualities - humility, listening, patience, courage - need personal growth as you step into your next chapter of leadership?

Chapter 15

Community Renewal

Theme: Communities strengthen when individuals and systems rediscover connection and shared purpose.
Purpose: To show how the Triad guides renewal in neighborhoods, agencies, and civic systems.

Opening Context

Every community reflects the relationships that sustain it. Streets, programs, and policies are surface expressions of something deeper, the network of human trust beneath them.

During my time with the City's Office of Homeless Prevention, I learned that outreach was never about simply solving problems, it was about understanding people. Each person had a different puzzle to solve, and my role was to help find the missing piece. Some pieces were housing, others were trust, and others were simply hope. The work always began with the same question: *Who stands before me?* Without that understanding, no service could reach them.

Healthy communities grow from respect, understanding, and cooperation. When people see one another as part of a shared "we," solutions multiply. When they remain disconnected, problems deepen.

Core Concept

Community renewal expands through three concentric circles:

1. Individual Renewal (Who Am I?)

People examine personal biases, values, and roles.

2. Relational Renewal (Who Are They?)

Neighbors and groups learn one another's experiences and needs.

3. Collective Renewal (Who Are We?)

Shared purpose directs collaboration and civic identity.

Progress emerges when these circles support one another.

Understanding Community Through the Triad

True community requires:

- Self-understanding

- Curiosity about others

- Shared ownership

When these align, communities gain resilience.

Application and Practice

Neighborhood Dialogues
Invite diverse groups to share hopes and concerns.

Agency Partnerships
Collaborate around intersection points:
> "Who are we to those we serve?"
> "Where do our missions meet?"

Puzzle Piece Approach
Every person has a missing puzzle piece. Community grows when people help each other find and place those pieces.

Shared Purpose Initiatives
Build around collective goals: safety, dignity, opportunity and connection.

Leadership and Community Perspective

Leadership is not limited to elected officials. Parents, volunteers, workers, business owners, educators, all shape community identity.

Communities weaken when people withdraw. They strengthen when individuals take responsibility for presence, compassion, and cooperation.

Community renewal begins with the shared question:
Who are we when we come together?

Summary and Anchor Thought

Communities heal when awareness expands, empathy grows, and neighbors work together. Renewal begins not with programs, but with people.

Anchor Thought:

"A community becomes stronger when its people remember <u>we</u>."

Reflection

Communities are shaped not only by systems and structures, but by the people who show up with care, intention, and presence.

Pause and reflect:
Where can you strengthen connection where you
live or work?
What small act of compassion or involvement might help
rebuild trust in the spaces you call home?

Communities grow whenever even one person leads with
awareness and empathy.

Chapter 16

The Mentor's Cycle

Theme: Mentorship is the living continuation of the Triad.
Purpose: To show how reflection, empathy, and collaboration form a repeatable framework that shapes future generations.

Opening Context

Every generation learns not only through information but through imitation. The behaviors, attitudes, and values of mentors become the quiet curriculum of every learner. Mentorship is not about tasks; it is about transmitting understanding.

The Triad provides the structure for that transmission: *Who am I? Who are they? Who are we?*

Who am I keeps the mentor grounded.
Who are they ensures the learner is seen as an individual.
Who are we forms the shared purpose that sustains progress.

Mentorship becomes a cycle: reflection, relationship, and release. When done well, both mentor and learner grow.

Core Concept

Mentorship moves through three repeating phases:

1. Reflection - Who Am I?

Examine motives, strengths, fears, and purpose.

2. Relationship - Who Are They?

Listen deeply. Notice strengths, patterns, and potential.

3. Release - Who Are We?

Share ownership. Encourage independence. Multiply leadership.

Every cycle ends by beginning another. Wise mentors remain aware that not every motive brought into a relationship supports growth. Clarity protects both teacher and learner.

Reflection Journal
Before guiding someone, ask:
>"Why am I offering guidance?"
>"What lesson am I still learning?"
>"How will I practice humility?"

Listening Framework

Follow the 70/30 rule:

listen 70%, speak 30%.

Co-Development Agreements

Begin with:

"We are here to learn from each other."

Teach the Triad

Encourage mentees to reflect on self, understand others, and contribute to community.

Release & Recognition Ritual

Celebrate transitions:

"What have we each learned?"

"How will you pass this forward?"

Leadership and Community Perspective

Mentorship connects generations, cultures, and professions. It builds sustainable organizations by developing people rather than positions.

Communities thrive when mentorship becomes a shared norm: older adults guiding youth, professionals guiding volunteers, neighbors guiding neighbors.

Mentorship is leadership multiplied.

Summary and Anchor Thought

The Mentor's Cycle ensures the Triad lives beyond one person or moment. It transforms insight into legacy.

Anchor Thought:
"Mentorship is leadership multiplied through understanding."

Reflection

Mentorship is not a one-direction journey; it is an exchange that shapes both the guide and the learner.

Pause and consider the people who helped you become who you are: those who listened, challenged, taught, or simply stood beside you.

Ask yourself:
Who might be waiting for your guidance now?
What wisdom, patience, or experience can you pass forward so someone else can step into their future with clarity and confidence?

Every act of mentorship extends the human connection we all depend on.

Closing Reflection

Connection is both a practice and a promise.

When we listen before we speak, when we act with purpose
beyond ourselves, we carry the Triad into the everyday
fabric of life.

Unity grows through small choices, quiet moments when we
choose presence over distance, curiosity over assumption,
and courage over silence.

Every day offers a chance
to strengthen "we."

Afterword
The Continuing Question

Every book ends, but understanding does not. *Who* was never meant to give final answers, it was written to renew the question. That question begins each day before any title, role, or responsibility. It shapes how we lead, how we listen, and how we live.

Writing this book returned me to moments across my career: crisis calls and calm negotiations, quiet conversations on cold sidewalks, families searching for connection, people fighting to hold on to hope. Different places, different people, yet the same pattern remained: when we take the time to understand *who* stands before us, the noise fades, and connection begins.

The Triad is not a concept to memorize, it is a rhythm to practice.

> Reflection reveals identity.
> Empathy reveals humanity.
> Cooperation reveals purpose.

When these move together, individuals find integrity. Organizations find trust, and communities find hope.

The Triad belongs wherever people work to understand one another; at a kitchen table, a boardroom, a locker room, or a civic meeting. And it belongs especially in moments when division feels easier than dialogue, or when assumptions seem simpler than awareness.

There is a phrase I learned early in my military service: **"Divide and conquer."** It was a strategy built on weakening the other side through fragmentation. Over the years, I watched that same pattern play out in families, workplaces, neighborhoods, communities and our government. Division makes us smaller, weaker, and easier to break. Polarization is simply division amplified, and it reshapes who we are until we no longer recognize ourselves.

Division is not just a social fracture; **division is identity erosion.** It pulls us away from who we are, distorts how we see others, and destroys the space where unity grows. If we are to be strong as people, as teams, as communities and as a country, we must choose connection over separation. We must decide *who we are* together, not apart. Unity is not agreement; unity is commitment. And it remains the strongest force we will ever have.

Gratitude strengthens this commitment. It reminds us to honor the people who shaped us, the experiences that taught us, the struggles that refined us, and the connections that carried us when we could not carry ourselves.

Gratitude grounds identity, softens perception, and deepens unity by reminding us that none of us grows alone. When we practice gratitude, we protect the Triad from erosion and see more clearly: *Who am I? Who are they? Who are we becoming?*

Carry these questions forward, not as tasks, but as companions. Wherever you show up, bring the courage to see others clearly and the honesty to let them see you just as clear.

Final Anchor Thought:
"The question of who is not about identity alone; it is the compass of every relationship and the path toward a more connected world."

Epilogue
Carrying the Question

Thank you for taking this journey through the Human Relations Triad. My hope is that these ideas meet you where life unfolds, in everyday decisions, conversations, and quiet moments of reflection.

The Triad belongs wherever people seek understanding over assumption. If you carry anything from these pages, let it be the habit of asking *who*, of looking for the person before the position, the story before the judgment, and the shared purpose before the difference. Each time you do, the bridge between "I," "they," and "we" grows stronger and the world becomes a little more human.

"Divide and conquer" was once a strategy of war, but in modern life, it becomes a strategy of separation and polarization.

- Division without question makes us vulnerable.

- Unity makes us resilient.

- Division is identity erosion.

- Unity is identity restored.

And unity emerges through presence, humility, and the willingness to see one another as human first.

Gratitude secures this unity. It challenges us to appreciate where we've come from and who has helped us along the way. Gratitude is a quiet thread that holds relationships together, reminding us that none of us grows alone.

Carry these questions forward:

> **Who am I?**
> **Who are they?**
> **Who are we becoming?**

Wherever you show up with your time, your voice, your presence; bring the courage to see others clearly and the honesty to let them see you just as clear.

The question continues, and so will you.

Epilogue Anchor Thought:
"Division erodes identity; unity restores who we are."

Acknowledgments

Writing this book has been a journey shaped by decades of service and by the many people who trusted me with their stories. Each moment, whether in uniform, in outreach, or in quiet conversation, helped form the foundation of the Human Relations Triad.

To the mentors who guided me, the colleagues who challenged me, and the friends who supported me through every season of growth: thank you. Your examples of leadership, humility, and service continue to influence how I see the world and the work ahead.

To the individuals I met through crisis negotiation, law enforcement, and homeless outreach, your resilience taught me more about human connection than any textbook ever could. Many of you may never know the impact you had, but your stories live deeply within these pages.

To those who served beside me in Florida's elder and community services: your dedication to dignity and compassion remains a steady reminder that "we" becomes possible only through shared purpose.

To my family, who stood with me through long nights, long years, and long journeys: thank you for reminding me who I am when the world grew loud and gray.

And to every reader who chooses to carry the question *who*: if these pages help you see yourself, others, and your community with deeper clarity and humanity, then this work has fulfilled its purpose. Thanks!

With gratitude,
D. W. Yonce

About the Author

D. W. Yonce (Dennis W. Yonce) has dedicated more than forty-five years to public service across military, law enforcement, emergency response, and community advocacy. His career began in the United States Air Force, where he served as a **Law Enforcement Specialist** and first learned the importance of seeing people clearly, especially in moments when clarity is hardest to find. He continued that commitment to public safety as an officer with the **Hollywood Police Department**, later joining the **Ocala Police Department**, where he rose through the ranks and served in multiple leadership roles.

Alongside law enforcement, Yonce was a certified **Emergency Medical Technician**, responding with firefighters and paramedics to support individuals in crisis. These experiences deepened his belief that effective service requires presence, steadiness, and a willingness to meet people where they are.

After retiring from the Ocala Police Department, Yonce continued serving the community through the **City's Office of Homeless Prevention**, helping individuals experiencing homelessness navigate complex barriers in search of stability. During this work, he learned a profound truth: **every person carries a different puzzle, and no two missing pieces are the same**. Some needed housing, some needed trust, some needed hope, yet each needed to be seen as a whole person before meaningful change could occur.

He also worked with dedicated volunteer teams protecting the rights and dignity of Florida's senior population, reinforcing his belief that advocacy begins with listening, understanding, and honoring the humanity of each individual.

These combined experiences, military service, law enforcement, crisis response, mentoring, outreach, and advocacy, shaped the development of **The Human Relations Triad**, a framework centered on identity, empathy, and unity. Throughout his career, countless individuals returned to share how his guidance and presence impacted their lives, affirming the enduring influence of service rooted in compassion and respect.

Today, through Triad Leadership Press and SilverLink Navigators, Yonce continues mentoring leaders and community advocates across Florida, helping others rediscover connection through one essential question:

Who?

Final Reflection

Understanding "who" is not a destination; it is a way of moving through the world.

Each day invites us to: look inward with honesty, look outward with respect, and look between us with empathy and trust.

The Triad grows stronger every time we choose responsibility over avoidance, communication over silence, and unity over division.

Pause here, at the end of these pages, and consider the small acts of awareness that have shaped your own journey.

Where will you bring more presence?
Where will you listen more deeply?
Where will you speak with greater courage?

And who will you become next as you carry these principles into your life, your relationships, and your community?

The question continues, and so does your path.

Closing Anchor Thought:
"Who we become is shaped by how we choose to understand."

Your Notes

This is your journey, capture what matters.

www.ingramcontent.com/pod-product-compliance
Lightning Source LLC
Chambersburg PA
CBHW052137270326
41930CB00012B/2926